I0645486

FARHIA YAHYA

& other short tale
and poem

Dedication

To those who always intend good, whether that materializes or not. To those who keep their hearts clean, whether they struggle with that or not. To those who are always searching for their higher and more righteous self.

Keep going.

Contents

Madness 11

Come Inside 13

From a Balcony 14

The Burden of Growth 16

The soul's need to breathe 17

Inertia 19

The Woman with the Crossbow 21

Punctuations of life 22

Beautiful Lies 24

I is for Ithar 25

Wasting away 28

The Midnight Rider 29

Close your eyes, feel your feet 30

A delicate balancing act 31

Prayer Mat 34

Trapped 35

Tell them it's a beautiful world 44

Only a Mother 45

Bed of Thorns 47

When all is over 48
Like Gold 49
A walk down the pebbled path 51
The Room 52
Because you aspire 57
The Man and his Neighbour 58
The Thief of your Soul 61
Mirror 62
The Fly 64
Home of Peace 66
The Father-Daughter Talk 67
Your Potential 71
Joy is around you 72
Unresolved 74
Familiarity 76
Elusive 77
A Detox 78
Under the Great Oak Tree 80
Purple Hue 88
Love is a child 90
On the Mend 91

"And they give preference over themselves, even though they are in need…"

- The Qur'an 59:9

Foreword

'I is for Ithar' is a collection of fictional short stories and poems at times told in a fable-like manner. *Ithar* is an Arabic word which means to prefer something over oneself for the greater good – an act of selflessness. It comes from the root word *'athar'* which also means to leave a footprint or trace.

It's my hope that the tales and stories written here inspire us to cultivate the selflessness that lives within us, and we leave a mark in this world for time to come.

MADNESS

"What are you doing, grandma?" The little girl asked.
"I am planting something, my dear." she replied.
"Oh. Is that why you always carry the water-can?"
"Yes. I like to spend some time under this sun and tend to these crops here."
"Erm, does it take you long, grandma?"

At this, the elderly woman turned to the young girl and smiled. The memories of many years flashed in her eyes and she paused. "Does it take me long? Well, I've certainly lived a long time, my dear, but no this doesn't take me long at all. Here, come closer, I want to tell you something."

The girl hurried over and sat very close to her grandmother.

"Sometimes, my dear, you have to stop in your steps and remember to live your days. Lift your head and see the sky. Turn your gaze and take in your surroundings. When you smile, give that smile time to form, if you are hurt, give your pain time to heal, and when you're happy, give your joy time to live fully."

"I think I understand, grandma," she said with an understanding nod. "When I play, I don't think of anything else but playing. And when I cook with mummy, I don't think of anything else but cooking with mummy. I remember all these moments really well."

"I know sweetheart. That's because those moments live in your heart, as you have lived them. Old people like me have a lot in common with children like you. We both take the time to live in the present and we cherish it. But soon the years will come, and you'll forget this skill of yours. You'll be chasing pleasure and not find it. You'll be chasing time and not have it. You'll be chasing many things and not realise that they live in a time-zone that you'll have long forgotten to live in - the present."

"That's madness, grandma."

"And life has driven many people mad, my dear."

COME INSIDE

Every once in a while,
You need to retreat indoors.
To the warmest and cosiest parts
Of your home and heart.
To heal,
To nourish,
And regain what the world has stripped you of,
Or taken away from you,
Or stolen from you.
Retreat, to remember who you are.
To find the missing pieces,
To the puzzle that is your life.
Come in and take off
Those coats of burden,
That God never placed on your shoulders.
Retreat, because sometimes, my friend,
That's how a glorious victory comes.
Remember the army that retreated
Only to launch back and win the war.

FROM A BALCONY

From the balcony she saw it all. The heated arguments between loved ones, the lonely man in his garden, and the wanderer on the street. She saw the hardworking newsagent opening his store at the crack of dawn just as well as she saw the busy mum dropping her kids to school - but unbeknownst to the world, she had also been up at the crack of dawn.

She saw the trees that died and the trees that lived, the dreams that transpired on the streets, and the dreams that slowly died upon them. She saw those who walked with clear purpose or need, and those who walked ever so reluctantly home. She heard life all around her; sounds of joy and sadness, of busyness and boredom, of movement and silence - indeed, silence had a piercing sound too.

However, she stayed on her balcony. Although life was beautiful, it also scared her. It meant she would have to take her place on the streets below and experience as others experienced. It meant living through all that she saw engulf others and it meant risking above all, her vulnerability. Life demanded openness. And that was something she had yet to open herself up to.

But a balcony is still just a balcony, not a detached realm in a parallel universe. And so, the owner of the newsagent store waved the morning paper at her asking, "Are you going to collect this, or shall I send the boy around again?". The busy mum ran across the road with the children, and she threw a smile at her as she passed underneath the balcony. The wandering man nodded in her direction and the fighting spouses paused for a moment before the husband looked up at her and threw his hands up in the air. "'Ere, talk to her please, maybe she'll listen to you…" he said defeatedly before walking back into the house.

Life called for presence and as much as she wanted to stay up on her balcony, as much as she wanted to hide, one way or another, life continued to beckon her and bring her back to the world below.

THE BURDEN OF GROWTH

Said one seed to another seed, "I shall sprout, grow tall, and overshadow you till nothing of light reaches you." The other seed replied, "Be careful the sprouting doesn't kill you first. How many seeds fail to flourish because they underestimated the immense pressure of growth and overestimated their ability to endure. Success shakes the hand of the humble and turns away from the face of the haughty and conceited."

THE SOUL'S NEED TO BREATHE

Drawn by the enchanting aura of the circles of knowledge and driven by his need to breath in this world, he wove through the ancient market as a man on a mission. Nothing distracted him from the haste he now made - not the flutter of colourful silk fabrics, nor the sweet smells of jasmine, brewing coffee, and succulent cuisines.

With a book under his arm wrapped in muslin, he rushed like a madman in a desert; thirst threatened to kill him so he rushed towards what his father used to describe only as 'springs of water' and 'a fountain of life.' How he wished he had listened then.

At a wooden door, he knocked and waited.

"Enter in peace!" someone cried from behind. He pushed open the gate and humbled his head, 'As-salamu `alaykum' he greeted. A chorus came back, 'Wa 'alaykum al-salam' and he breathed in the atmosphere. He used to hear that Angels roamed these places, but a life of recklessness and wretched disregard made him dismiss anything and everything

that he didn't see with his eyes or didn't land a coin in his pocket. But the stories must've been true because although he saw no Angel, he stood gazing at angelic souls from the entrance of a wooden gate that was closed to a bustling world outside and open to a soulful one within.

"And a wall will be placed between them with a door, its interior containing mercy, but on the outside of it is doom." [al-Hadid: 13]

He took his place in this sea of faithful believers and passionate hearts and began to open his book in haste when he felt the gaze of someone on him. He looked up to see his teacher wearing a warm smile that said only one thing: "Open your heart first, dear son. Always open the heart before the Book, and the Book will be opened to you."

He took a moment and breathed at last, before hearing the turn of a thousand pages and the voice of a single scholar.

INERTIA

"I only wanted to help him," Musa said with a sigh.

He was in the staffroom at school with a colleague who was now sitting down beside him nodding.

"That's a great thing," his colleague said. "Really, it is. But how did you actually try helping your cousin?"

Musa narrowed his eyes at him. "Come on, you know I've tried. I've told him countless times to get his act together. I've given him resources and shown him the best way forward but he's just so resistant to anything I say. God, it's frustrating!"

"Inertia." His colleague whispered to himself.

"Come again?"

"Erm, inertia? It's a law in Physics about resisting a change in motion."

"And what does that have to do with anything here? I mean, I know you're a Physics teacher, but seriously...?" he raised his eyebrows playfully.

"No, I was just thinking. You want your cousin to start moving in a new direction. But any time there is a change in motion like that in Physics, inertia will set in and resist the change temporarily. I think you should give your brother some time. Let him start moving slowly until he can gain his momentum. We often want everyone to move with speed in new directions – but the Laws embedded in this world point to otherwise."

"Hmm," thought Musa. "That's interesting."

THE WOMAN WITH THE CROSSBOW

"Double cross me once, and I will forgive." She said as she peered at her opponent through slanted and unforgiving eyes. Her bruised cheek now writing a new history between them. Trust tired her out sometimes.

"I will forgive from my heart," she continued as she wiped her forehead, tired from the battles and wars, "But I will learn and observe; all the steps you took and all the paths you traversed. And I will never fall prey again."

For a moment, a flicker of a new and almost deadly emotion passed through her eyes. "For I will be a master of the roads through your jungle, the strings of your web."

And just like that, she lowered her crossbow and arrow, all her defences, and walked off with all the strength she could muster.

PUNCTUATIONS OF LIFE

"But why am I seeing this again?" Jawahir said almost in a whisper. It was the second or third time she was coming across it. She turned to her cousin with pleading eyes. It wasn't that she was scared by the coincidence, no, she was beyond fear altogether. She simply just wanted to escape the maze, the endless questions and dead ends.

"I don't know what to say, Jawahir," her cousin replied as she pulled down the curtains over the bay windows that invited so much blinding light into their living room. "Sometimes, things come back in our lives, I suppose."

"But why, Yumna? I've been racking my brain over it for the past week."

Yumna cast her eyes down and busied herself with stacking books on the shelf. Finally she said, "Maybe, maybe it's because you didn't notice it the first time as it ought to have been noticed. Maybe you didn't learn from it when it came as a teacher, or maybe you didn't thank and embrace it when it came as a gift. The oceans throw out their pearls to the persistent divers, Jawahir. Maybe what we miss, we see again in another form, and we think it's a new matter. But it's just a continuation of what was before. Life returns many things to us, sometimes so that we can overcome past pains, or learn to trust again after losses.

Maybe Jawahir, it's come back to put a full stop where you've been putting all those commas and question marks."

BEAUTIFUL LIES

A lie is still a lie even if a crowd of thousands chant it, and truth is still a truth even if one lone voice whispers it. Some people are talented in the way they tell you their story. Beautiful words adorned with false sincerity. Their lips tell the tale in a calculated and timely manner. Like a garden that's watered just at the right time. Their tongue sows a seed whose fruits you just don't know of yet. Magical and yet unsettling, you find yourself falling for the story, time and time again. Their eyes play a part as they flicker and prey on your vulnerabilities. Watching your every move and reaction; they are ready to chop and change the story to entrap you further and make you believe. They're talented because they've done this before, and you are not their first victim. Nor the last.

But a lie is still a lie even if you desperately want to believe it. Even if it's charming, it's still unsettling. It troubles something deep within your heart. You want to believe it, but you know something's not right. Set yourself free with an ugly truth instead. Please set yourself free.

I IS FOR ITHAR

"I hope," she said as she planted the seed, "that this will cool someone's eyes one day as much as it cools them from the sun." And with that, she walked on until she came across a collapsed tree.

Without hesitation, she put her saddle bag on the grass and began lifting the heavy branches one by one, removing them away from the path. "I hope this will ease someone's travel as much as it prevents them harm," she whispered.

When she saw an orphan boy staring at the juicy sweets through the shop window only to dig into his pocket and find nothing, she hastened into the store and bought those very sweets. She handed him his treasure, patted his head too, as the warmest of smiles formed on his face and a tear strolled down both their cheeks. "I hope," she said to herself, "that he will grow up and be inspired to cause many a smile on the faces of others."

Wherever she went, her mind was active; seeking the ways that she could better all the things around her. There was never a smile that she didn't return, hardly an outstretched hand that she didn't reach back out to, and never a plea for help that she didn't respond to. She lived the Prophetic narration that *"God is helping His servant so long as the servant is helping his brother..."*

This was the secret and also the answer to the questions that multiple people asked her when they would exclaim, 'How are you so strong? How are you so independent? How is it that you never seem to need people?!' The truth was, she was always in need. But her needs were well and truly taken care of.

Her name was Ithar... Arabic for selflessness. She embodied the powerful concept of preferring others over oneself and in turn, she basked in the divine care of God Himself.

She was a bit like space.
Silent and glittering but moving worlds inside.

WASTING AWAY

Rise above it all.
The drama, the hate, the arguing,
the time waste.
Pick your battles but realise
that even in those you pick - you don't always have to be
an active soldier.
Rise above the pettiness of others.
Seek your own path and know
when they drag you into their drama,
they're dragging you more and more

...away from yourself.

THE MIDNIGHT RIDER

Like a twinkling star and a distant oasis. Like a fading dream and a faint memory. She remembered her goal. Her wishes. Her dreams. They were what had kept her up at night as she pleaded in fervent prayer, and during the day, they were what preoccupied her mind. She planned this goal so meticulously and made sure she strove every day to achieve it.

But time wore her down. Days turned over on her. Obstacles stood in her path. People mocked her. So, it became a like star. An oasis. A dream. And a memory... All unreachable.

But on that particular day, or was it a night, it came back to her like a midnight rider. It returned to her heart before it returned to her mind. The star suddenly became vivid and bright. The oasis drew closer. The dream materialised. The memory became set in stone. She knew her goal was now just a reality waiting to happen.

Night wrapped its cloak over the world as she lay her head on the pillow... "*Insha'Allah*, tomorrow I shall try again," she said. "By God, I shall try again."

CLOSE YOUR EYES, FEEL YOUR FEET

"And that is how the Scales balance out," she said.
"What do you mean?" the young girl asked.
"The days will merge into each other and bewilder you such that you cannot tell one from the other. But when you look back after a year or a decade, you see that the days were so different."
"So, you're saying that I should take each day as it comes?" the girl asked.

The woman paused before looking up at the girl. "I am saying that you are in the eye of a storm right now. Don't be afraid to close your own eyes in order to get a sense of your bearings and to gather your strength so that you can see and feel your surroundings despite the whirl of the hurricane.

The easy days and the difficult days are but two sides of the Scale, so understand fate, my dear. Understand the Decree."

A DELICATE BALANCING ACT

Said one teardrop to another, "I am made of the good stuff." The other teardrop looked over and stifled a laugh. "You do know that we're made from the same components, you and me? We came out together."

Just as the teardrop uttered those words, a giant glass pipette loomed over them and sucked them up. The scientist in his laboratory with his ridiculously bright coat now had both drops in his grasp and was hurrying towards a microscope being careful not to lose what was to be his greatest discovery. He quickly dismissed the young volunteer who was evidently the provider of the tears. The young man collected his belongings – photos, videos, and a joke book of all things! – and quietly left the lab.

Using extreme care and delicacy, the scientist placed both drops under the greatest scrutiny of their lives and before long, a sudden but joy-filled 'Eureka!' filled every corner of the lab. The teardrops were indeed made from the same components – the good stuff as one of them claimed – but neither knew just how unique they were.

"Why is the white-coated man jumping for joy?" one of the teardrops asked. The other turned to face him but just before it could respond, they saw tears coming out of the scientist's eyes. A gasp could be heard from under the microscope just then as both teardrops looked up in amazement. For the tears that now came gushing out from the scientist's eyes were none other than their fellow brothers.

Excited and besides themselves, they shouted, "Over here! Over here!" But their brothers did not hear them. Instead, a reply came from behind. "Don't get too happy, they won't be joining you." The teardrops swivelled around and froze. "Who are you?"

"I am tears of sadness... made from the not-so-good stuff." His gloomy humour couldn't even make him laugh. "Your brothers as you call them, are not part of the investigation like you are. Like I was, and like we were." He gestured over to the side of the worktop and the fresh young teardrops gasped once more as their gaze fell upon on rows and rows of tears - all different shapes, sizes, and intricate details. They didn't recognise any of them.

As if reading their mind, the sad tear said, "This is grief," and he pointed to the nearest teardrop to him, "I feel like he understands me the most and I could swear I've seen him before." The tears of joy looked towards grief, then at sadness, and then back at grief. Yes, they detected an undeniable similarity between them, almost as if they were cousins or unidentical twins born within a short time of each other.

"This is stress and over there in the corner is anger. They are both quite volatile, mind you." Sadness then turned back to the teardrops of joy and seeing how young they were and lacking wisdom, he said, "And you are tears of joy. You're quite contagious. Never forget your worth, little ones."

They didn't know it just then, but every tear, every single one them had a unique design – released by a unique emotion. Grief was not the same as joy, nor was anger the same as pleasure. Each had its own chemical make-up; its own story which brought it into the world.

"You see, it's a balancing act," the sad tear said, as if on cue. "The pent-up emotions of people need to be dealt with, and we are what balance the emotional scales. We are delicate, but our job is magnificent. We are the telling of a beautiful story and every one of us will have his day."

PRAYER MAT

"I understand now," he said as he sat on his prayer mat. He understood and was in awe. Nothing had gone his way, but a warm feeling spread within his chest. His efforts had seemingly amounted to nothing and the people pitied him but for once this didn't knock him. He knew the Hand that moved this universe was the Hand that turned his life.

"Failure" they said. But in a world where every day was another chance to make an effort, 'failing' seemed almost natural. In a world where we've been given the Divine instruction to 'Work!', 'Make effort!' and 'Try again!', failing didn't seem so scary but merely just part of the journey.

"Fear not the people, but fear Me." [al-Ma'idah: 44]

"I understand," he said again, as he realised the absence of fear in his heart was what allowed the warm feeling to spread. Slowly, he got up from his prayer mat, folded it away, and walked back out into the world. Fearless and with an acknowledging heart, he was now unstoppable.

TRAPPED

The eastern market was unusually busy on this dusky evening. The sun had turned an eerie but beautiful colour of lilac and burnt orange, as if water-coloured in the heavens. Under an old palm tree, Kyrush peered through the cracks of an ancient wall at the unsuspecting merchant. 'Oh yes,' thought Kyrush as the rich merchant walked by with his almost-royal stride. His lush garment draped around him and the turban that nested on his head was made of the finest material. Lord only knew what treasures lurked behind that storehouse of his. Excitement began to take over Kyrush; he had been waiting for this moment ever since he heard the merchant was coming to the village square. Armed with a clever mind and some help from a fellow friend, his plan was set.

Kyrush stepped out from behind the wall and walked over to the merchant. Clearing his throat, he began, "Good afternoon, sir." The merchant turned around and beheld the young man. Surprisingly, he had a kind face. Wrinkles at the corner of each eye gave the merchant's face an effortless and resident smile. Kyrush felt unsettled.

"Good afternoon to you too. How can I help you, my son?"

"I heard you are the merchant from Andalus. What did you bring?"

"Well, that depends on what you're looking for. Sorry, what was your name, son?"

"Kyrush," he said absentmindedly as he stooped down to pick up a bottle of rich *'itr* (oil-perfume). Next to the precious oils were the finest cotton he'd ever seen. Excitement and fear both gripped him at once, he couldn't fail this mission of his. "How much can I buy this for?" he asked the merchant.

"Hmm, it's a reasonable price. But let me show you something else that might interest you." The merchant stepped to the side and behold, beautiful silk shawls were spread out in a multitude of colours behind him. As if in a trance, Kyrush walked over and ran his finger along the silk shawls. The soft material almost melted in his palm. He had never held something quite so spectacular.

Not wanting to waste any more time, Kyrush looked over to the ancient wall and gave an ever so slight nod, noticeable to no-one but him and his partner, Locin, who stood waiting behind the wall. He turned his attention to the merchant and asked for two silk shawls. "Golden," Kyrush added. The merchant smiled and nodded slowly. He turned to retrieve them when suddenly a man dressed in long dark garments with his face obscured, leaped forward towards the stall and grabbed the expensive perfumes before making a mad dash out.

"Hey!" shouted the merchant. "Thief! Thief!" he screamed. Commotion immediately set in and several merchants began to also shout. One poor merchant, evidently alarmed, dropped his clay pottery out of surprise! Kyrush joined in the outcry and began flaying his arms wildly at the merchant. "Catch him! Don't let him get away!" The merchant peered at the thief who was now running almost out of sight. "Quick!" yelled the people of the market. The merchant turned to Kyrush and said, "My son, I entrust you with my store till I return." He then rushed and made way after the thief. Kyrush smiled and nodded.

The merchant gave chase to the thief, and they moved through the market like cat and mouse. The merchant no longer shouted after him. He was simply hot on the heels of his evader. Locin was now running with the oil-perfumes, excited by the idea that he was able to outrun the merchant if he wanted. He was obviously more youthful than him and quicker on his feet. But the plan was specific. He wasn't to outrun the merchant, instead he was to be far ahead but still visible, then feign taking an alley marked by Kyrush where a trap awaited. Locin snickered and made haste, looking over his shoulder now and again. But Locin was a dreamer and every so often he would catch himself lost in thought. He rebuked himself to stay focused. After all, he only has one job to do and that's to stay ahead of the rich old merchant.

Kyrush felt all the eyes of the market on him. He couldn't make his move just yet. Instead, he pulled a stool out and sat at the entrance of the stall, showing everyone that he was indeed fulfilling his promise. The storehouse loomed behind him, and he felt its luring call. For days, he wanted to access it, but the merchant never left its side. Except for today. Patience was key and Kyrush was determined to play his cards right.

About a quarter of an hour had passed and everyone seemed to return to their stalls. No-one looked to him anymore and the usual hustle and bustle returned to the market. Kyrush looked left and right. He was too nervous to move so he waited some more. He looked one more time to make sure, then he got up slowly, stretching and slyly looking around again. Taking a deep breath, he quickly made his way around the stall and towards the entrance of the magnificent storehouse. It resembled a marque but much grander. As he walked in, darkness engulfed him, and it took a few seconds for his eyes to adjust. He made his way around old pieces of clothing and worn-out containers and then found himself facing a door. This was it. For sure, treasure lay behind this door. All those days of planning now paid off.

Kyrush calmed his beating heart and took a few breaths to steady himself. Then he pushed open the door. The first thing he saw was the lush red Persian carpet; a breath-taking splash of colour and comfort. On the walls, lanterns glowed, and incense burned away in the far corners. A grand Arabian majlis surrounded the Persian rug. Kyrush was dumbstruck. A majlis?! A council?! Where were the rows and rows of rich possessions he heard about? Where was the treasure?!

"There's nothing here my son." A voice said behind him. It struck Kyrush down like a lightening bolt. He spun around to see when lo and behold, he saw the merchant seated at the corner of the majlis. His head - now bare of a turban - was lowered in deep thought. Kyrush's heart immediately began to pound.

"Oh, erm, old man, there you are," he laughed nervously. "I was wondering what happened to you. Did you catch the thief?"

"I did not need to catch him. Just like you did not need to send him."

Startled, Kyrush began his defence, but the merchant waved him off and stopped him in his tracks.

"Do you know what they say about the plotter?"

"Err, I wasn't trying to, erm, plot anything," he began but again the merchant cut him off.

"It says in the Scriptures of old that whoever digs an evil hole for his brother, will end up falling into it himself."

Kyrush froze and the back of his neck startled to tingle. How could this old man have known anything of his scheme? And where was Locin?! His mind flew into an array of questions, but no answers came. He kept silent and the merchant continued.

"Beware of the traps that your soul sets when it's hungry or deprived. Be even more wary of the extent to which the *nafs* will go, Kyrush."

Kyrush was in two minds. If Locin had been caught, then there was no use in lying. But if he had gotten away, then how could the merchant know? He decided to come clean.

"How did you know, old man?"

"Everything about you gave it away. Your eyes, your twitching finger, and even your feet showed me a man on a mission not a casual man of the market."

Kyrush peered at the merchant as if trying to decipher his words.

"You showed your lust for this world and disregard for yourself when you gave the oil-perfumes more attention than you gave your own name. You simply handed me your name instead of introducing it to me. You showed your short-sightedness when you bought the silk shawls instead of the fine cotton, when, in reality, you are more in need of cotton than fine silk. I was testing you, you see."

"Kyrush, you told on yourself long before you told your companion thief to come out. And that was just the beginning of your downfall." He went on to tell him about Locin's fate, how he took the wrong alley, most likely absentmindedly, and fell into the trap set by Kyrush.

Kyrush could barely stand any more. He grasped a wooden bar to his left. Slowly, he lowered himself to the floor. The merchant had seen right through him. Shockingly, he observed and knew more about Kyrush than Kyrush did himself.

"Kyrush, this world is tough, but it has a passionate dislike for the deceiver. It prefers the innocent fool to the fanatical schemer. Don't you know that it's written in the scrolls that, 'As you treat others, you shall be treated, and the cup you give to others, is the cup you shall drink from?'"

Kyrush finally spoke from his humble new awareness, "Teach me," he said.

"My son, I can show you, but I cannot teach you. Instead, I will tell you this; clean out your heart even if it leaves you utterly vulnerable and become an eager student of life – she has always been your teacher."

"What do you need?" they asked.
"Only the Mercy of God." He replied.

TELL THEM IT'S A BEAUTIFUL WORLD

Tell the elderly they are valued,
And tell the young of their newly gifted canvas.
Tell she who doubts herself that intelligence is hers,
And tell he who is cautious that courage lives within him.
Tell the fearful children that the world is kind – don't destroy it for them so soon,
And tell the exhausted parents that no-one could've done it better than them.
Tell the ill some stories of hope and Paradise,
And tell the lost that they'll always find their way back home.

Remind them all that it's a beautiful world even though everything around them may point out otherwise.

ONLY A MOTHER

There was a deep sadness that no-one knew of, and she made sure to hide well. But her mother looked at her from across the kitchen island and it was a look that penetrated her deeply. It was seeking answers to questions that could never make it past the throat. She pulled her fleece over her arms tightly because the look made her feel uncomfortable and yet she needed it. She needed someone to invade her spirit, her soul, and force out a voice; an answer. Only a mother had the power to do this. Only a mother could stare into your soul and provoke the deep within.

Without saying a word, her mother turned back to washing the dishes. Silence fell between them, and it wasn't long before her daughter fidgeted in her seat and cleared her throat.

"Mum, can I get your advice on something?"

Her mother smiled to herself as she closed the tap and put the dish on the rack. Her instincts were right, and she had done this a thousand times in a thousand different ways. The intuition of a mother is a powerful thing.

"Of course, my dear," she said as she turned around to face her daughter. "What's on your mind?"

And just like that, the deep within was awoken.
The dam broke.
Her daughter spoke.

BED OF THORNS

He knew it was a mistake. But that's the funny thing about emotions; you get lost in them and forever regret what comes next. In the heat of the moment, whether it's anger, desire, fear, pride, or reckless behaviour, you lose yourself. He couldn't catch himself in time. And so, he fell into regret. A young lad laughed at him on the street corner. How can you laugh at the fallen, he thought to himself.

It was then that a voice was heard calling in the distance, "Don't mock the sinner for his sins and ascribe to yourself false piety. For God often accepts the fallen and rejects the arrogant for his lack of compassion."

WHEN ALL IS OVER

When all is gone, and all is over
When the dust settles
and all is buried
you realise
not everything had to be said.

and some things
were really not that bad.
But emotions severed tongues
and also made tongues
As if they were saws
and double-edged swords.

So in the end, everything died.
Killed.
Murdered.
At the hands of mere words.

LIKE GOLD

"From a thousand stories, I found myself. I read Your Words and they spoke to me like the ancient-old inscriptions they were – more ancient than my soul – telling a tale of my own. Like a sweet song ringing to the tune of my life; like a strong rhythm sounding to the beat of my own heart.

They ask me, 'What happened to the locks on the hearts of the people?'
'Hardships came and unlocked them all,' I replied.
'What brought the hardships to the town?' they asked.
'Neglect of His Word,' I replied.

They shook their heads and walked away, no wiser then when they first approached. 'Hold on!' I cried. 'Every verse will elevate you in more ways than you can know, in more realms than you realise.' But they looked at me like a lunatic whose words were worthless.

My words are indeed worth nothing, dear Lord, but Yours are priceless. They remain among a people who struggle to tell what's valuable from what's counterfeit.

But the reader knows as every letter envelops him that it will squeeze. Till like gold, he shines from the inside."

A WALK DOWN THE PEBBLED PATH

"No," he whispered to himself. "I shan't." And so he turned his back. With determined steps, he began to walk away, down the pebbled path which was neatly lined with messy shrubs and tufts of grass.

An old woman who sat across the road winked at him as he walked past her. Years of experience shone from her face as deep ridges and wrinkles engraved into her skin like a maze, telling the story of a lifetime - of loss and lessons learnt.

"Some doors are best left closed," she said. And he knew then that she wasn't just talking about the door he had almost opened and dared to go through.

THE ROOM

Noura walked in and saw nothing but four walls of concrete brick and an open floor. It reminded her of a fighting cage; two opponents enter but only one comes out in triumph. She walked in and sat down, cross-legged on the floor, head bowed down, waiting.

'Bang!' The walls shook slightly as her opponent threatened to tear down the entire room. But today, she wasn't here to fight. Nor was she going to flee. She was done with all that. Noura was here to finally confront and try to resolve. See, her opponents today weren't strangers, but rather residents of her soul. They were her emotions and feelings, and for the past few decades, they had become so tangled up within her that she no longer recognised what was what. She had begun reacting without thinking and was sad without tangible cause. She cried herself to sleep or found herself driven towards making decisions out of desperation and kept people at bay. A voice kept telling her that this would only get worse unless she stepped into the room. And so, here she was, waiting in silence to see who turned up.

At first, her opponent was silent and still, staring into her soul. Then it drew closer and closer. It was hooded and it was fiery; its eyes glared in sheer anger. But Noura kept still. She looked up and locked eyes with what was evidently her own anger. No running away, no deflecting, and no riding the rollercoaster she knew too well. Instead, she held the ground for once and faced this head on. Anger spoke to her in a blazing voice, telling her of days long past, of things she had forgotten. But she kept silent, and she observed. She listened intently and soon the voice lost some of its fire. She acknowledged the story, acknowledged the pain and slowly the voice calmed down. She accepted and nodded each time as anger brought up everything that kept causing the eruptions over the years. Noura blinked slowly and looked to the floor.

"Now, do you understand?" It finally asked. "Yes, I do." Noura replied.

"Thank you." Anger whispered, now calmer than before, to the point that it could barely be described as anger anymore, and it made its way to the door and left of its own accord. It had finally felt understood.

But then Hurt walked in. Noura looked at it with surprise. She was not expecting it, and like the stranger that she saw it for, she asked, "Where did you come from?" Hurt was forthcoming, thankfully.

"Remember that day when you were betrayed but you said you were fine? You were not fine at all. Remember when your beloved made that comment, and you laughed but really, you wanted to cry? Remember when you were younger and looking forward to that event only to be overlooked and shunned by your peers, how deep it cut?" It spoke and Noura dug deeper. After so many revelations, of unrecognised betrayals, of being ignored, and of dashed hopes, she now understood this feeling that lay behind anger. They spoke for a while until it too quietened down and left the room, having gotten everything off its chest.

Soon after Hurt disappeared, Fear entered the room. It had a flicker to it; at times it seemed dark and at times it was impulsive and volatile. The unpredictability of it scared her, but Noura stayed and did not move. Just as she did with the others before, she listened, acknowledged, and reassured. She continued this process of hearing out all the feelings and emotions that came. For fear was followed by resentment which was followed by stress which was triggered by rejection that was caused by unrequited love. She realised she was working backwards.

One by one, she untangled it all. Each time the feeling was acknowledged and understood, it left the room at a time of its choosing. And each time it did, Noura felt weight being lifted from her shoulders. Things were untangling right before her. She kept working through it all and the process took her deeper and deeper until a last knock came to the door. 'Strange,' she thought. None of the others had sought permission. Noura walked over and opened the door. It was a little girl. Of course, it was none other than her inner child.

Noura crouched down and put her hand over the little girl's heart. "I'm so sorry," she whispered. The little girl reached back out and held Noura's face in her small palms. "I forgive you," she said with a smile forming. "It's all going to be okay now."

A foot that slips is a foot that learns where to step next.

BECAUSE YOU ASPIRE

Do good deeds not because you are righteous, but because you want righteousness to enter your heart.

Give in charity not because you are rich, but because you are truly poor in the Eyes of God.

Love and seek the good in others not because they treat you well, but because it's your nature to love and not hate.

Live and do things because you want to be a greater person not because you currently are.

Aspire for what's higher, loftier, and mightier
Because that's the world where your soul is from.

THE MAN AND HIS NEIGHBOUR

Once upon a time, a man was visited by his neighbour who was a very talkative man indeed. One could hardly get a word in whilst talking to him! He would describe every aspect of his story and give you every detail of his imagination. The men and women of the streets were much entertained, but his neighbour was not. He was long suffering and had had enough of all the chatter. It almost drove him insane.

The man did not have the patience today. He was hosting an old friend of the desert. A nomad who spent most of his life waking up to new landscapes each time under a different sun. These days of travelling made him into one of the wisest men he knew.

'Knock, knock!'

Slowly, the man opened his front door and saw standing there none other than his chatty neighbour.

"Greetings!" the neighbour said hurriedly with a warm and excited smile. "Oh, I'm so glad you are home. I heard your voice from over the garden and just had to come and see you. It's been a while. Where have you been? You didn't answer the door the other evening and last week too, your wife said you were sleeping. I was worried something had happened to you! But I'm glad to see you are well. Oh, I see you have a guest? A nomad! Greetings, O friend of my neighbour. Care if I join you? Oh, you must tell me about the desert..."

In one breath, the neighbour had singlehandedly invited himself into the man's home and it wasn't long before he sat between the two men conversing like a young child.

The owner of the house became tired and weary and looked over to his guest with sorry eyes. He had told his wise friend about the neighbour, but he didn't have the heart to tell the neighbour about himself. Truth was, sometimes his conversations were uplifting like the time he was sick, depressed, and just wanted to fade away. His neighbour had been God-sent with his creative tales. But most of the time they were a burden. He didn't know what to do. For sure, this would annoy and upset his guest.

The wise man glanced at his sorrowful friend and then peered at the chittering neighbour. Taking a breath, he finally interrupted the dialogue.

"So, you want to know about the desert? I'll let you in on a secret. I met an explorer one day on the coast of Kismaayo. I heard he wanders through these cities too. He has with him vessels of every type of sand that he collected as he traversed two continents and more." The neighbour's eyes lit up. You could almost see a world of incredible beauty begin to construct in his mind. "He mixes them in the most extraordinary fashion; layers and layers of colourful sand, sparkling and twinkling. Some say they shine in the hands of the true explorer. The sand grains are so rare because they are from lands no man has ventured into before."

"O nomad! Pray do tell, where is this explorer?" asked the neighbour.

"Well, I heard he is passing through the market today. If you are quick, you just may catch him."

"Oh!" The neighbour squealed with delight. He quickly turned to the owner of the house and gushed out, "I must go, please excuse me!" And with that, he rushed out of the house and hurried down the street towards the village market.

The man looked to his guest in wild bewilderment. But the guest, being a man of experience and wisdom simply uttered an age-old proverb from the lands of Somalia, *Nin tag lama dhaho lakiin wuxuu ku tago ayaa la tusaa* - "You do not tell a man to 'go away' rather show him that which will make him go of his own accord."

THIEF OF YOUR SOUL

Some things are really not that deep. Nor do they deserve that explosive reaction, or deep attention and all that energy. Before you react to something that's just happened, close your eyes and consider; is it something necessary or rewarding? Is it coming from a place of sincerity and God-consciousness, or is it coming from a place of greed and anger? Will it matter tomorrow, in the next month, or towards the end of your life? And where do you think it'll place you in the life to come?

If you think these questions are way too deep for the situation, then it's obviously not a situation deserving so much depth of your soul.

It's a thief.

MIRROR

You are loved
even if you refuse to love yourself.

And your presence is cherished
even if you can't be by yourself.

You are missed
even if you are the one who ran away.

And you are welcome
even if a thousand times you feel like a stranger.

You are strong
even if you've crumbled at every step.

And you are beautiful
even if you can't look in the mirror.

You are protected
even if you can't see your guardian angels.

And you are sought out
even if you pick yourself last.

You are funny
even if only a few laugh at your jokes.

And you are smart
even if no accolades line your shelf.

You are you
even if you try so hard,
so desperately,
so cunningly,
to be someone else.

Sincerely,
Your faithful mirror

THE FLY

"Today, I killed a fly." Adam said as he sat on the bench with his finger digging into his thumb. Him and his wife were both watching their 6-year-old twin boys play football in the park. "All my life they said I couldn't hurt a fly, but today I killed one intentionally."

"Did you set off to kill it?" His wife asked?

"No."

"Did you wake up today desperate to slaughter a fly?"

He chuckled. "No, of course not."

They were silent for a moment before he continued, "Funny that. You can be seen in one way and have a reputation all your life, but in a split second you become something else."

"Are you seriously telling me that taking a swipe at a fly made you into some deep, intelligent person now?" His wife said as she elbowed him playfully in the ribs.

He smiled then sighed. "No, but you don't understand how angry I got at this tiny, insignificant thing. It kept flying into my face, trying to get into my coffee mug, and it wouldn't leave me alone! The thing is, I didn't think I could actually hit it. Then in a moment of sheer mania and anger, I lashed out and that was the end of life for this small bug."

"Hmm, well I guess everyone has a limit eh? Don't worry yourself too much. I'm sure there are still billions more to populate the planet! Come on, let's kick some football with the kids."

At that moment, just as Adam was about to get up and jog over to the twins, just as he was about to dismiss the happenings of his day, a fly flew over and landed next to him. It stood still and Adam was left in thought. He watched it as it scurried to the side of the bench and then lingering for a moment, it flew over his mug. As if on cue, it then flew into his face which startled Adam. He began to feel a sense of irritation again. The same emotions were starting to rise in him once more.

But this time, he knew he had a choice. He wasn't going to allow something so insignificant to have such an impact on him. He decided to let go and see the fly for what it truly was; a small matter in this big arena we call life.

We are all surrounded by flies... Those matters that beg for attention and provoke that craze within us. Some people give in and react, and some choose to see the insignificance of the fly in their life.

HOME OF PEACE

Peace be upon the afflicted who cry in pain.

Peace be upon the lonely who wander in vain.

Peace be upon the fatigued who struggle through today.

Peace be upon the confused who can't find their way.

Peace be upon the broken-hearted whose tears flow.

Peace be upon the oppressed who lack the freedom to grow.

Peace be upon the soul who deals with blow after blow.

The Home of Peace awaits you, in all its glory and glow.

THE FATHER-DAUGHTER TALK

Marriage. It was a topic Ayman knew was coming. He had sons and daughters who were bound to walk through its circle, and he hoped he had raised them well enough to not only coast it, but to thrive under its shade.

"But I love him," she said through sorrowful eyes.

"Love alone is not enough, my dear. No matter how many people tell you otherwise, no matter how many movies reel it off as the moral of the story. The reality is that marriage needs more than just love to maintain it."

"Well, it needs at least 90% of it," Ayah whispered as she crossed her arms over her chest.

"Whatever it is; 90% or 50%, the reality is that love can come and go in any relationship. It may be strong one year and fall in embers the next, followed by a rekindle. The key is that despite its ups and downs, you have more than just love that holds you together."

Ayah sighed and shrugged. She knew this conversation wasn't going anywhere. But her father always had a point. She looked at him and her eyes wandered to a canvas on the wall. It was a photo of the southern beach they visited years ago. Pebbly shores led to a turquoise sea and a wooden pier stood to the side. The canvas was a happy memory of when they were a young family, before everyone grew up and things became distant.

"True love is peaceful." Her father continued. "It doesn't call for drama, hostility, or the need to cling so unhealthily. It's like an ocean which at the surface may become rough, tidal, and unpredictable, but it always has a calm undercurrent to it – a world where things live in unison and harmony.

My dear, you need to know yourself very well before getting to know another person. You need to acknowledge your emotions and know when to restrain them and when to let them free. You need to be your own guide. Allow your head to lead you, let it secure a healthy environment for you, and then your heart will bask in the security and enjoy the fruits. Keep an open mind but also keep your wits about you. They say that people are as different as the fingers on your hand, and not every glove will fit."

"Seek out the kind and caring, the considerate and sensitive soul who has strength of character, piety, and the capacity to love you with his soul. Not everyone has the capacity to love beyond their own self. True love is serene, and it should put you at ease, not keep you at the edge of your seat. So, pay close attention to anything that troubles you deep inside; watch for the story that doesn't make sense, the hair that curls on your skin, the shiver that comes without warning, and the window that opens through a person's eyes."

"Know your worth and seek your equal. Someone who matches you, not on superficial levels, but at the levels that mean the most to you. And for that, you need to know yourself well. If you cherish truth and honesty, then seek the truthful but if you cherish only the beauty of this world, then you'll fall for it at every turn."

"Take your time because time reveals the hidden man. Be wary of anyone who rushes you beyond your comfort because God loves steadiness and haste is the devil's tool. All good things will come into fruition and remember that fate cannot be rushed before its moment."

"My sweetheart, joy can come to a broken heart that's moving on. But it seldom comes to one of broken principles. So, seek a pious and principled man and you won't ever have to worry about ill-treatment. Seek the one who chooses right over wrong, who chooses your happiness over his convenience, who chooses mercy that favours you over justice that serves him, who chooses to consider you in his smallest decisions, and who protects you even if that comes at his own demise. Choose him who chooses you – the real you that you may keep concealed from others. Don't settle due to your fear of a broken heart and don't settle due to the fear of not finding someone else. Just as fortune favours the bold, love favours she who lives her life fully and meaningfully."

"Oh, dad," sighed Ayah as she buried her head in her arms. "You are right. You are so so right."

YOUR POTENTIAL

Spring. It is a season from amongst the annual seasons, but it also means to have the ability to return back to shape. To return to normality. My hope for you is that you spring back from every winter that visits you and you blossom after having lost your leaves; your smile, your confidence, your strength.

The more a spring is pressured, the greater its potential energy. So, the more you're compelled or coerced by life, or burdened, or made to coil under its immense tension, the greater shall be your emergence.

What may feel like you having all your energy depleted, is in fact you getting ready to spring back – with an explosion of hidden and stored energy.

JOY IS AROUND YOU

As she vacuumed the living room, the sun's rays shone through the high windows and fell on the plush grey carpet. It instantly warmed up beneath her feet and she soaked it in. She couldn't wait for Summer to kick in – her favourite season! The town would soon come to life, the trees would sing again, and the days would rapidly become long and drawn out with the beauty of festivities.

She dusted, polished, and tended to her morning routine. She packed everything away and lit some scented candles before making herself a warm cup of coffee and relaxing on the sofa for a few minutes. She breathed it all in and felt the comfort seep in through her skin. How she loved her home; her serenity and place of joy. Her uncle once said to her, 'Find your joy; even in the mundane.'

Her two little children ran in moments later. Laughter and little squeals filled the room as they leapt into her arms. She buried her head between them blowing raspberries against their soft skin – sending them into fits of laughter. Their tiny hands hugged her tight and their little feet used her as a climbing frame.

Nothing could be more mundane than sweeping and tidying a room, followed by tending to children. Yet nothing brought her more pride than this. She loved her world, and her world gave her more to love.

Find the joy in your mundane.

UNRESOLVED

"What are you doing?" asked Zainab.

She had that teenage frown on her face as she watched her mum crouching down by the front porch and peering between the bushes and flower stalks. A gush of water flowed in a nearby fountain, the drops glistening under the morning sun.

"Hmm," said her mum. "It looks like a spider built her home here. That's a shame, I must've unwittingly encouraged it with this shade I constructed last week. Funny that."

"What's funny about it?"

"Well, we never quite know what happens as a consequence of our actions, do we?"

Zainab scoffed, half expecting a speech indirectly telling her off, but to her surprise her mother continued in a low tone, almost talking to herself.

"Our lives are all linked and intertwined, much like the strings of this cobweb or the stones on this pavement or the drops of water streaming down that fountain. We breathe in as others breathe out, we come through doors as others leave through them, and we speak as others take a pause. Even our tests start where others end theirs."

Zainab looked at her mum with a reflective gaze. "Do you think children also pick up where parents stop?" She asked with a gleam in her eye.

Her mother paused and stared at the ground. Then she sighed and looked away. "My dear, children have long been picking up from where their parents forgot to heal."

FAMILIARITY

The familiar sounds of the vibrant market rang out all around him, but the man did not stir. He slept on with an old tarbush hat resting on his face as the trading city of Marrakesh burst with life. Pots and pans clanged, women laughed in a corner, and hagglers and merchants engaged in loud and often animated bargaining. Every few seconds, a motorcycle would go past with its revving engine as men shouted from stall to stall. But still, the man did not stir.

We rest best in familiar environments and funnily, we get accustomed to things which were once strange or quite bothersome! Loud noises bother those who derive energy from the stillness whilst silence can bother those who feed off the bustle around them. It is whatever you've accustomed yourself to so take care of your surroundings, your company, and where you place yourself.

It eventually becomes your source of nourishment.

ELUSIVE

If it were something you could fix,
You would've done your darn best to do so.
But how can you fix anything,
If you don't know where it broke?
The issue evades like nothing before.

But the world is round,
And what escapes often comes around.
So, watch your back,
And watch your ground.
Be still, let it all catch up.

T'is true for not just karma, but also deep lessons,
What goes around, will come around.
And pay heed to the essence,
Because when life opens her hand, she presents the elusive,

But often not in the way you expect.

A DETOX

Sara watched the steam rise from her cup of coffee as she sat alone in the warm café. It was just after 11am and things had quietened down from the morning rush. The snow from last night had settled on the ground, painting the town a brilliant white, and the air was now crisp outside. It was a bright and beautiful day, a blank canvas almost, but she couldn't appreciate it as her head hung low, her eyes to the floor. She felt so alone.

"Is this seat taken?" A voice called beside her. Sara looked up to see a middle-aged woman with a purple jacket and matching scarf around her neck. She recognised her; it was her aunt Suzie.

"Oh! Auntie! How are you?"

"I'm alright, dear Sara. I thought you'd be here. How are you? I heard about what happened."

"Yeah, story of my life eh," Sara responded back faintly. For a moment, she found herself back in her thoughts over issues she was facing, replaying scenes in her mind. She sighed and took a sip from her coffee. "The drama was just too much, auntie. But now I feel nothing. I feel empty with nothing around me. Everyone and everything has just disappeared."

"Aww, I know, my baby" her aunt said as she leaned over to squeeze her arm. "But you know, perhaps it's been emptied for a reason."

Aunt Suzie had an understanding smile as she peered over her glasses.

"What do you mean?" asked Sara.

Aunt Suzie raised an eyebrow as she drew her chair in. "Well, we tend to absorb too much of our environment, you see. So, sometimes God removes everything around you, and you're left with a blank that feels like bleak nothingness."

She smiled again.

"See it as a form of detox."

UNDER THE GREAT OAK TREE

With his hair in cornrows and wearing his favourite jacket, Kamal had a spring in his step as he walked through the vast nature reserve park behind his house. The sun was still out, and he was enjoying this stunning autumn weather. Walking through the park today was like walking through a watercolour painting; bursting with the warmest colours that he had ever seen. Admittedly, it had been a long day, but it was a productive day nonetheless, and it just made him feel good all around. Deadlines were finally met, he caught up with overdue work, and he even had time to prep for next week.

Looking to take a bit of rest, Kamal decided to sit down under a large oak tree. Some people said the tree was over a thousand years old. It did look ancient with so many deep ridges in its bark, and its tough trunk and crooked branches reaching so high into the sky. In contrast, it was surrounded by well-maintained green shrubbery. Kamal breathed out gently and closed his eyes as the tree shaded his face gently. He found himself slipping into a light nap when suddenly the noise of snapping twigs woke him up. He glanced to his left but there was no one there. 'Hmm,' he thought to himself, 'probably just a bird.' He closed his eyes and tried to doze off again. After a few minutes, he was woken up again but this time by a squirrel. Kamal jumped in fright as the squirrel froze just a few feet in front of him.

'Woah,' he said with a coy grin. 'You gave me a scare, you little thing.' The squirrel blinked but it did not move. 'Strange,' thought Kamal, as squirrels usually make a mad dash for it as soon as they spot a human being. This little one was being oddly brave. Kamal shuffled his feet towards the squirrel to scare it away but still, it did not move. He waved to it but again, there was no sign of it going. Finally, the squirrely slowly looked to the shrubbery that grew next to the great oak tree.

As if on cue, Kamal also looked over and it was right about then that he saw the most magnificent thing ever. He wasn't sure if it was the setting sun reflecting its rays off the leaves, but behind all the green, right there on the grass just a metre or so to his left, he saw piles and piles of gold coins.

Stunned, he did a double take and looked again. Why would there be gold coins scattered under a shrub? 'What a strange day this is,' he said to himself. He crawled over and picked up one gold coin. Wow, it was real. And it was heavier than it looked. He picked up another piece, and another, and even saw a few silver pieces all lying there on the soil. Kamal scratched his head and looked to see if anyone had accidentally dropped them or lost them. His eyes searched the park, but no one seemed to be in the reserve that day.

'It's all yours,' a small voice cried out. Kamal shot a look over his shoulder but there was no one there.

"Who said that?" He called.

"It's me," the voice said. "Hello. The squirrel in front of you? Yes, over here." The squirrel sat back on his hind legs, "Please, no screaming."

Kamal almost fell backwards. "You seriously didn't just speak!"

"I did. And I am telling you that this is all yours."

"How?!" Kamal asked regaining his composure. Then he shook his head before spluttering, "I mean, why?!"

"Well, you deserve it. You've always been such a hard worker even if you've not always been recognized for it. But I'm here to tell you, your efforts have paid off."

Kamal scoffed. He couldn't believe it. He didn't know what was more baffling, the squirrel or this treasure with his name on it, all underneath a bright setting sun. A million thoughts came into his head, but it truly felt like his lucky day today.

"How many coins are there?" he asked.

"A thousand," came the reply. Kamal smiled and grinned from ear to ear. "This is too good to be true."

"Well, it's yours to take or leave." The squirrel said ever so nonchalantly.

"Yeah, well... I guess I'll take it?" He laughed and shook his head in disbelief before gathering the coins and putting a few in his pocket. Should he count them or...? No, they looked like a thousand pieces. Kamal let out another laugh and flung his arms in the air in jubilation. "I can't believe it!" He yelled into the park.

An old man with a walking stick then came down the dusty path. Kamal quickly hid the treasure with his jacket and sat back under the oak tree. He smiled at the old man who slowed down to catch his breath.

"Are you alright there?" Kamal asked.

"Oh, I could be better," the old man replied. "I've lost my ticket home and now I don't know how I am to get back." His eyes looked lost, probably from wandering the park looking for his lost ticket.

"Why don't you just buy a new one?"

"Because I left my wallet at home," he sighed.

Kamal looked from side to side. He still had a few gold coins in his pocket. "Well, I guess I could help you with that. Here's a coin to help you on your way."

"Oh!" the old man cried, "That's terribly kind of you, young man, I don't know what to say. Thank you ever so much." The man's eyes were now filled with relief as he hastened on his way out of the park.

Kamal sat back, the leaves crunching under his feet. He leaned over to look back at the shrubs with his favourite jacket sprawled over the soil. Any other day, that would've annoyed him seeing his jacket get dirtied like that. But not today. Today, it covered over such wealth that could buy him a hundred jackets!

He began to fill his pockets with the gold coins when he heard the sharp shrill of a bicycle bell. He turned to see a young girl with tears running down her face. She slowed as she saw the squirrel standing there, resting on his hind legs. She rubbed her eyes as she drew to a stop.

Turning to Kamal she said, "Is he your pet?"

"No, I've only met him today actually."

She sniffled and looked down.

"What's the matter there," Kamal asked with a caring and inquisitive look. "Why are you crying?"

"Everybody at school was mean to me today." Fresh tears came to her eyes.

"Oh, there there now, sometimes kids say things they don't mean."

"No, you don't understand. It was a party, and I had no nice clothes to wear, nor any presents to swap with others. I was a laughingstock turning up bare handed!"

"Where are your parents? You really shouldn't be by yourself in this big park."

"My mum is nearby," She said as she sniffled, "But she's feeling guilty for it all."

"For not getting you what you want?"

"No, for not being able to stretch our means."

Kamal dug into his pockets. He had a steady job, but he knew very well what it was like to not make ends meet. Those days weren't far behind him. "Here, take these to your mother and keep this for yourself." He winked kindly as he handed over a handful of coins. The young girl's face instantly lit up with surprise and sheer joy. She squealed happily before thanking Kamal and dashing back up the path with her bicycle.

Kamal smiled as joy entered his heart too. It was indeed a strange day, but he shrugged and returned to the oak tree. However, just as he suspected, it wasn't long before another stranger came down the path. Kamal was a deeply reflective person and to him, this was no coincidence. Perhaps this treasure came with responsibility. Maybe the path of the wealthy was a path of service.

One by one, people of different backgrounds and needs came by him. Sometimes they were suffering and sometimes they were looking after someone in need. Others faced great loss, and some were burdened by matters of urgency. All turned to Kamal in what seemed to be sheer coincidence but in reality, was simply fate's tale. He kept giving away the gold coins and he did not stop giving. Until he had none at all.

In the end, he felt a bit sad but as he sat back, happiness took root in his chest – like the old oak tree took root in the ground. He had given away his treasure without having had the chance to enjoy it. But he was filled with happiness he couldn't explain and gratitude that came with every breath. Picking his jacket off the ground, shaking off the autumn leaves, he swung it over his shoulder and decided to make his way home.

He had forgotten all about the squirrel who was now stepping out from behind the shrubbery. It blinked twice and smiled slowly as he hurried to catch up with the young man to tell him again, that a treasure was all his.

It was indeed a strange day because right there in the shrubs, under what was now, an emerging moon, lay a treasure so vast with his name on it. This time it was multi-folds more than it was before... because charity never ever diminished one's wealth.

It only ever increased it.

PURPLE HUE

It was said that you could see them on the corner of Twelfth Street. But when I got there, I found nobody. It was strange because many people swore they were there, and an equal amount of society were convinced they did not exist. The debate raged about the people who walked around with a hue of purple emanating from them.

I came to see them and even question them; what is this strange colour that walks with you? But I found no-one. As I turned to walk back, I saw a familiar face from town, and we stopped to talk. We spoke at length and conversed like friends until a man walked past and nodded to my friend.

Do you know him?" I asked.

"Sort of." She replied, looking down on the floor.

As he walked off, I thought I saw a glimmer of colour on him, but it disappeared as quickly as it had come. 'Hmm,' I thought. I turned back to my friend who was now staring at me intensely. I caught a sad look in her eye. "What is it? I asked. She sighed and looked down the road. "He is one of them," she said, "He has the purple hue."

I gasped and looked at the man who was now far down the road. But there was no shade of purple anywhere. "You won't be able to see it," my friend said almost reading my mind. "It's a mark of loss and only those who've suffered a deep loss can see it. We share the pain, you see."

"Incredible. So, everyone who's lost a loved one has this hue of purple? And they can see the same on others?"

"That's right."

"Goodness. I'm sorry for your loss," I said, looking down to the floor.

"And I'm sorry too," my friend said as she squeezed my hand tight.

I didn't understand it then, but two weeks later, I received a call which turned my world upside down.

LOVE IS A CHILD

The candle flickered, its shadows dancing,
The meal stood ready; its steam entrancing.
The sun was setting, its rays bowing down,
The day was finally taking off its crown.

And the couple sat across the table from each other.

They joked and laughed; their faces animated,
They jabbed and made fun – so well acquainted!
But they were quick to sulk or pout so swiftly,
And just as fast, they would make up so softly.

Strange was this couple; they're usually so reserved.

One looked at the other, searching for reassurance,
The other gave it freely, it was mutual assurance.
A moment passed, and it seemed the table turned,
Now he needed assurance… how quickly one learned.

It was a learning curve; bizarrely learnt years ago.

It was strange to watch; they were quite child-like,
But isn't childhood where we first feel love's strike?
We're showered in it, from both mother and father,
We revel in it, grow with it, and give it to each other.

Love is a child, and become one you may be,
So, tend to your loved one as you would tend
…to your baby.

ON THE MEND

As heartbroken as he was, the father of two pulled himself away from the couch and tried to busy himself in old hobbies he once had. Since becoming a widower, life had no taste. It was pain infused with grey bleakness, but everything was telling him to get unstuck. He was trying. For the past week, the more he engaged in activities, the more ease he felt – although it was a challenge at times.

"How are you feeling this morning?" It was his mother speaking. She hadn't left his side for months since his wife passed. She finally left after he insisted but was back again within a few weeks. In her heart, he was still her young son, and now a grieving one.

"I'm better, mother." He said on the autopilot response he had become accustomed to. "I'm attempting to get back into the swing of things. You know how it is." A faint smile appeared on his face.

"That's wonderful, my dear. You are going to be alright."

The young man looked away. It seemed like everybody kept repeating the same thing – that 'he was going to be fine' and 'everything will be okay.' A small sense of annoyance crept into him.

"Everyone says that, mum. But no-one really knows, do they? No two days are the same, sometimes I feel like I'm doing fine and the next I'm not! It's like I'm going crazy. So, if I don't even know how things are going to be, how can anyone else?" He sighed and dropped the screwdriver he was holding. His mother tucked a stray grey hair behind her ears and gently picked up the fallen tool. "My son, you're going to be alright and I'm sure..."

"How, mum?" He interrupted her, raising his voice slightly. This wasn't like him at all, but grief was a monster that brought out inner monsters.

His mum looked at him intently before handing him the screwdriver. "Because" she began, "of all the 'hobbies' you've had, I've never seen you so engaged in this one before." And with that, she walked out of the room. He looked down at his hands and realised what she was saying. He was holding the screwdriver in one hand and a broken picture frame in the other. The table in front of him had an array of items; mostly broken possessions he'd found in the house. But on the right-hand side was the most intriguing thing – a set of newly mended items.

He was absentmindedly fixing the broken, and in the process, he was fixing himself.

Every footstep leaves its mark; just like every soul leaves their story behind.

www.ingramcontent.com/pod-product-compliance
Lightning Source LLC
Chambersburg PA
CBHW010547100726
47902CB00008B/2113

* 9 7 8 0 9 9 5 6 0 4 2 2 3 *